Getting Ahead at Work Without Leaving Your Family Behind

Joy!

by
Bonnie St. John

Bonnie

Published by:
St. John Deane, Inc.
315 S. Coast Hwy. 101, Suite U-94
Encinitas, CA 92024

Copyright ©2001 Bonnie St. John
All rights reserved. No part of this book may be used or reproduced, stored in a retrieval system or transmitted in any form or by any means: electronic, photocopying mechanical recording or otherwise without the written permission of the Publisher.

Inquiries should be sent to:
St. John Deane, Inc.
315 S. Coast Hwy. 101, Suite U-94
Encinitas, CA 92024
www.sjd.com
(760) 944-7590

Printed in the United States of America.
ISBN 0-9707146-0-2

Contents

About the Author 5

Introduction 6

The Problem 12
Successful careers are tearing families apart.

The Solution: Blending Work and Family 16

Historical Background 20
How did we get into this mess!?!!

An Idealized Example 25
Florence Griffith Joyner, Olympic Athlete

Ten Principles for Blending Work and Family:

1) Your family's sanity starts with you. 32
   Susan Taylor, editor-in-chief of *Essence* magazine.

2) Make decisions jointly as a family 39
   Lebron Morgan, advertising executive for Black Entertainment Television.

3) Encourage each family member to explore their passion, skill and personality through their work 43
   David Alexander, Secretary of the American Rhodes Trust, former Claremont Colleges President

-3-

4) Involve Your Children in Your Work.............. 50
   Florence Griffith Joyner, Bob Chappelle, Laura Tyson, Ken Blanchard, & everybody!

5) Build team spirit into a family mission........................ 56
   Michael Osheowitz, Wall Street financial consultant. President of the Edwin Gould Foundation for Children.

6) Pace yourself.. 65
   Laura Tyson, former Economic Advisor to the President and Head of the National Economic Council in the White House.
   Ken Blanchard, author of *The One Minute Manager*

7) Use technology to defend home life, not invade it. 74
   Paul Zane Pilzer, President of ZCI Publishing.

8) Find an Organization which Supports Your Goals, Values and Family Life. 77
   Russ Karlen, Blue Diamond Executive for Nu Skin.
   Bob Chappelle, Corporate Training Executive for Saturn Corporation.

9) If you can't find a supportive job, create one................ 87
   Bonnie St. John, President of SJD.

10) Focus your efforts and your relationships................... 94
   Herb Kelleher, CEO Southwest Airlines.

Conclusion 100
Summary List of Principles..105
Acknowledgments..108
Additional Products..111

About the Author

Bonnie St. John is an international speaker, executive coach, and president of St. John Deane, Inc. An amputee nearly her entire life, she competed on the US Disabled ski team at the 1984 Olympics in Innsbruck, Austria and won silver and bronze medals. Since then, she has worked on Wall Street, lived in Europe and Asia, and earned awards as a sales representative for IBM. Bonnie was appointed by the President as a Director for Human Capital on the National Economic Council in the White House. She is a graduate of Harvard and Oxford, where she studied as a Rhodes Scholar.

Recently, *NBC Nightly News* featured Bonnie as one of the five most inspiring women in the nation. Her story of courage has appeared on the front page of the *New York Times* and *The Christian Science Monitor*. Television shows and magazines such as *Good Morning America, The Charles Kuralt Show, People Magazine, Ebony* and *Essence* have all featured stories about her achievements in sports and academics. Bonnie has spoken before corporations, associations, and community groups throughout the country, sharing her experiences and her techniques for achieving peak performance.

Bonnie lives in San Diego with her daughter Darcy where she runs her business as an inspirational writer and speaker. Bonnie's lecture topics include: *From Global Economic Trends to Personal Power; Teamwork Under Fire; Succeeding Sane: Secrets of Successful People Who Stay Sane*; and *The Art of Self-Motivation*. She is a contributing author to the book, The Winning Spirit, and is the author of Succeeding Sane, published by Simon & Schuster.

Introduction

"Balance" is not a helpful concept for anyone who has both ambition and a family. To me it conjures up the image of trying to get home by 6:00, cook dinner and give quality time to children when you feel like collapsing instead. It feels like you are failing your family. It feels like you are falling behind at work. How can you compete with people who stay until eight or nine pm, work weekends and never have sick children?

Balance is highly stressful. Working parents are left frustrated at work and unsatisfied at home.

> It is clear the future holds opportunities;
> it also holds pitfalls.
> The trick will be to seize the opportunities,
> avoid the pitfalls,
> and be home by 6:00.
>
> -- Woody Allen

I am so excited to have discovered the antidote to a balanced lifestyle: *blending*. The philosophy of blending offers a new vision.

Blending has freed me from the mental prison of mediocrity at work and at home. As you will read in this book, blending has profoundly affected the way I make decisions about everything including business travel, volunteer work, arranging furniture, and long-term career decisions.

I am anxious to shout this important message from the rooftops to anyone who will listen:

> Balance is a hoax!
> There is a better way!
> Free yourself and your children from balance-purgatory!

Okay, so I get a little carried away sometimes. I feel the urgency of sharing my new sense of hope as a human being and as a parent. Today, more than ever before, we have the potential to undo the damage done to our families by the industrial revolution without losing any of the technological gains. We can reclaim our lives and our families if only we learn to see our choices differently!

"We possess only
the happiness we are able to understand."

-- Maurice Maeterlinck

Let me tell you how I learned about blending work and family. This book fell into my life accidentally, like being hit on the head by a falling diamond.

I was researching, interviewing and writing for a book about the successful people I admired most. I interviewed people who not only reached the top in Olympic sports, in national politics or on Wall Street, but also managed to stay happy and healthy while contributing to society. It was not my intention at the outset to ask anything about family life or parenting in particular. I just wanted to know why a seemingly small number of people could achieve at the highest levels without being destroyed by it.

As I interviewed my friends and role models for *Succeeding Sane*, found many who could not talk about work without mentioning their children. It was so striking to me how many interesting family stories popped up that I put them together and analyzed the material. Successful men and women from completely different walks of life were saying the same things about their children.

I began to see the significance of this new way of thinking about work and family. As a new parent myself, it changed my life. The chapter kept growing until my editor put his foot down.

"It doesn't belong in the book anymore," he said.
"But it's my favorite chapter!" I responded in surprise and disappointment.

After we discussed it, however, I realized he was right. These ideas had taken on a life of their own which digressed too far from the subject of *Succeeding Sane*. The chapter had to go.

Once I accepted that the chapter on families would be cut from my book, I got excited about really giving it a life of its own as a separate, self-published booklet.

"This is so typical of you," a friend told me, "taking an obstacle and turning it into an opportunity. You just don't see problems, do you?" "No, I guess I don't," I laughed. "Cutting the family chapter from the main book turned out to be the best decision all around."

As a separate booklet, it will reach more of the working parents who urgently need to know. It will reach them sooner and at less cost than if it was a small chapter in a large book on success strategies. And that makes me happy.

If you want to learn the complete philosophy of blending, read about my life story, and use exercises to create a personalized plan for your personal and professional life, you will want to read *Succeeding Sane* published 1998 by Simon & Schuster. On the other hand, if you are primarily interested in using the concept of blending to ease work and family tensions, this booklet is the place to start.

If, after reading this booklet you also feel the urgency of letting other working parents know about it, give us a call and let's talk. [(760) 944-7590 or Bonnie@sjd.com] You can order more copies at a discount and give them away, you can write an article for your company or club newsletter, you can hire me to come and speak for a group. Or maybe you have better ideas.

I want to lead working parents through a wave of change; to rise up and claim their own greatness without sacrificing the children. Please feel free to join me.

Our deepest fear is not that we are inadequate.
Our deepest fear is that we are powerful
beyond measure.
It is our light, not our darkness
that most frightens us.
We ask ourselves, who am I to be
brilliant, gorgeous, talented or fabulous?
Actually, who are you not to be?
You are a child of God.
Your playing small doesn't serve the world.
There's nothing enlightened about shrinking so that
other people won't feel insecure around you.
We are born to manifest
the glory of God that is within us.
It is not just in some of us; it's in everyone.
And as we let our own light shine we consciously
give other people permission to do the same.
As we are liberated from our own fear,
our presence automatically liberates others.

-- Nelson Mandela
1994 Inaugural Speech

Joy is the feeling that comes from fulfillment of one's potential.

-- William C. Schutz

"Every year I live I am more convinced that
the waste of life lies in
the love we have not given,
the powers we have not used,
the selfish prudence that will risk nothing,
and which,
shirking pain
misses happiness as well.

No one ever yet was the poorer in the long
run for having once in a lifetime
'let out all the length of all the reins.'"

-- Mary Cholmondeley

The Problem:
Successful careers are tearing families apart.

Consider this story of a successful couple:

"I am a product manager for an Internet startup company and my husband is a management consultant. On a typical day my husband drops off the kids at a full-day, pre-school program. To make up for his late start, he stays later at work and gets home after the kids are already in bed. Every year his salary goes up and so does the pressure.

"I have an hour commute each direction in rush hour traffic-- a very stressful drive. My CEO has a wife and two kids who he seldom sees. He only takes off a little bit of Sunday. That sets the pace for everyone. If I didn't have kids, giving my life to the work could be exciting and stimulating. I feel like I need to have pride in what I do. I want to have a good job and work hard.

"But with kids I feel stretched to the limit. I know my kids are fine with excellent pre-schools and all the best care. But I want to be the person who answers their questions about values. They are interesting people and I want to be a companion. I don't want to let someone else have all that. Yet, I pick up the kids at 6pm and find that I am thinking, 'How long will it be before they go to bed?' I want to go to my room and be by myself for a little bit even though I have hardly seen them at all.

"I have lost more than the kids. I have lost a feeling of peace. I never, ever have time for myself. I don't have time or energy to exercise after fighting the rush hour traffic. The whole thing is pretty dissatisfying. I'm not doing well enough at work and I'm not doing well enough at home. I could do better if I just had a little more time.

"Then I start to question, why am I doing this? When two people like us have successful careers, the family could live on one salary or the other. You realize you are actually doing this out of choice. Are you getting back what you are putting into it? Are you really enjoying it? Is it socially meaningful? I feel pressure to quit my job and stay home, but that isn't me. I have no right to complain.

"We are so fortunate to have so much success in two careers and two wonderful boys. I know most people have much harder lives than we do with less money and flexibility. We are the model couple for success. Is this frantic, chopped up life really what I aspired to? Why?"

-- *(Name withheld by request)*

How can two people be so successful and wealthy, and yet so trapped? If you feel crazed and fragmented by a similar lifestyle, you are not alone. What hope does a family have when they only meet in the off-hours?

> "Tell me not in mournful numbers
> life is but an empty dream."
>
> -- Henry Wadsworth Longfellow

In response to this crushing pressure, many women and a few men are dropping out, downshifting, or otherwise giving up their external ambitions to salvage their private lives. "The poster girl of the 90's is the drop out mother," writes Susan Estrich for USA Today. "Forget about Super-woman; these days the woman on the magazine cover has traded in her briefcase and partnership for a diaper bag and a stroller." (If she can.)

But dropping out doesn't necessarily make women happy. Sociologists report that women are happier when they can have a career as well as a family. They are happier but more stressed. The average working mother reports a higher stress level than the men and women who work in occupations generally associated with stress: air-traffic controllers, police officers, and doctors. Mothers seem damned if they do work and damned if they don't.

Can you imagine an alternative to the typical life of a two career couple in which working parents can pursue their career goals and still have a viable home life? After interviewing over thirty of my role models it has become clear to me that the happiest of the high achievers have a very different image of family life. They really do live differently from the "norm."

I've arrived at the outermost edge of my life by my own actions.

Where I am is thoroughly unacceptable.

Therefore I must stop doing what I have been doing.

-- Alice Koller
in *Stop the Insanity*
by Susan Powter

The Solution: Blending Work and Family

Blending family with career ambition seems to have certain common elements regardless of whether you work in the White House, train for the Olympics or work on Wall Street. I have taken the comments I heard from very different sources and distilled them into the following ten principles:

Ten Principles for Sane, Successful Families

1) Your family's sanity starts with you.

2) Make decisions jointly as a couple or as a family.

3) Encourage all family members to explore and develop their passion, their skill and their personality through their work.

4) Involve your children in your work.

5) Build team spirit into a family mission.

6) Pace yourself.

7) Use technology to defend your home life, not invade it.

8) Find an organization that supports your goals, values and family life.

9) If you can't find a supportive organization, create one.

10) Focus your efforts and your relationships.

Each of these principles comes from the experiences of parents and spouses who are working in high-pressure occupations. When I spoke with these people, they all seemed to be saying the same things. The more I learned, the more I could see the simple logic of their approach to life.

Blending family with a competitive job hinges on one inescapable reality:

> Highly successful people in any field
> spend more than forty hours per week working.
> Thus, their only hope for having a good family life
> is to bring their spouse or children
> into the hours spent working insofar as possible.

Each of the people interviewed do this to a greater or lesser extent. Some have family around all the time they are working. Others have family around on a steady, but intermittent basis. This seems almost like common sense when you accept that excellence absorbs an awful lot of one's time and energy.

The premise of blending may be simple, but implementing it is not. You won't find in this book a cookie cutter solution that you can stamp onto your life. Nor will you find something that will instantly fix all your problems. All of the people I interviewed said that they have always wrestled with work and family issues and never completely resolved them.

Applying blending in your life requires an interplay between seeing the vision of a blended lifestyle and breaking it down into practical tools you can use to build your own. This book alternates between conveying the overall vision and providing specific "what to do next" ideas.

Certain elements of the book are designed to help you build up a gestalt sense of blending work and family. Only by understanding the big picture can you see why the ten principles are so powerful.

The next section deals with the big picture by putting it in historical perspective and showing why it seems so alien to us modern city dwellers. The section on Florence Griffith Joyner's family provides a story about an idealized blending situation.

Each of the family stories used as examples throughout the book should give you a different window for viewing the concept of blending work and family.

In addition to conveying a general concept or philosophy, I wanted to give you tools to use right away for putting blending to work for your family and career. This book contains ten principles that represent building blocks for creating this "blending" lifestyle. There are exercises at the end of each section to help you with each principle. At the end of the book you'll find a self-assessment section and a summary of the exercises in the book.

Many people say,
"Getting rich won't make you happy."
That may be true, but getting poorer
won't make you happy, either.

You have to look beyond
money, stuff, and racking up achievements to
be happy.
You have to pay just as much attention to
personally meaningful things like
integrity, parenting,
or developing your talents.

Go ahead and get rich.
But go after real happiness with equal zeal.

-- Bonnie St. John

Historical Background:
How Did We Get Into This Mess!?!!

Before I describe the examples of families that work well, I'd like to give you some historical background that puts this problem into perspective.

We often say that family life is disintegrating without realizing how important that description is. The life of the typical two-career couple is highly dis-integrated as in "disconnected" and "dis-jointed." The man goes to his company, the woman goes to hers, and the children go to school and/or daycare. They lead largely separate lives with little if any connection to one another.

Each member of the family is pursuing his or her life's work, mission, and what should be a passion, in complete isolation from the other members of the family. This is not sane.

Many people--including women--blame this situation on women who want to work outside the home. I hit the ceiling when a woman friend of mine explained to me that men going to work and women staying at home to look after children is the "natural" order of things. I knew that seemed wrong!

From that point of view, families were just fine until women went to work. The women's lib movement was at fault--so the reasoning goes--for encouraging women to desert their post as family stabilizer and enter the work force to compete with men.

You have to ask yourself, though, if families were fine, why were women so unhappy and feeling trapped? If families were doing fine, why were men walking out on their wives and children in record numbers? Why did so many men feel bored to tears by a woman who spent her entire life caring for his family and his home? This model for a family *was not* just fine as it was.

A recent *Fortune* magazine cover story cited several examples of career women who dropped out to save their family life (March 17, 1997: "Is Your Family Wrecking Your Career?" by Betsy Morris). One of them was Karen Sukin, a promising Atlanta lawyer on the partnership track who stopped working altogether after having her third child.

Meanwhile her husband, Brad, continued to work as a lawyer for 60 to 80 hours per week. He seldom ate dinner with his family and spent evenings and weekends networking to build his practice. Last summer he went five months without a day off. He became a partner in his law firm.

Although becoming a partner was what he wanted, it is a bittersweet kind of success. He and Karen feel their family life is not healthy. She misses the challenge of being a lawyer. He misses seeing his children and his wife.

I trace the roots of this family dis-integration back to the industrial revolution. Before the advent of big factories and big office buildings, it was no more natural for a man to leave home to go to work than it was for a woman to do so.

Before the industrial revolution, everyone had a home-based business. Farmers did. So did the blacksmith, the butcher, the baker and the candlestick-maker. Home was usually built next to, over, or within the space needed for baking, weaving, or growing crops.

As a result, most people could eat three meals a day with family even if their work required very early mornings or late nights of toil. When business was slow, there was more time with family and more leisure. In busy times, kids and spouse could pitch in and help.

Everyone shared the sense of achievement and pride in the "family business." Sure this is an idealized picture, but it has some definite advantages over the chopped up lifestyle of the modern, two-career couple. It's a different ideal of success.

The industrial revolution came along and spoiled everything. Big factories and later on, high-rise office buildings forced Dad to leave home every day, all day. Advocates of balancing work and leisure finally forced companies to accept the concept of weekends and eight-hour days so that families could have time together. Weekends as a concept weren't necessary when families regulated their own work and leisure balance. (Notice that I don't say work and family balance...there was no such distinction.)

In this strange, new industrial environment arose the motherhood role we now accept as "traditional." Mom makes family, kids and home her first priority. She may do some volunteer work or get involved in community affairs, but her primary responsibility is to the children and the running of the home. This allows Dad to go to work and take little responsibility for home life.

The industrial revolution completely destroyed the concept of a family working as a tightly integrated team for a shared goal. The new scenario separated "at-home" Mom with almost no outside career from "at-work" Dad with almost no home life. They had little in common.

During the 70's and 80's women ditched this definition of domestic bliss in droves. Some sought the challenge, the wealth, and the accolades their husbands received in the outside world. Some went to work to offset the rising costs of supporting a family. Others were forced as single Moms to become a working parent.

Both husband and wife work in 84 percent of married couples today.
--Besty Morris, *Fortune* magazine March 17, 1997

Kids spend significantly less time in the company of adults than they did a few decades ago.
-- Carnegie Council Report on Adolescent Development

"Kids are highly stressed. If parents don't give them enough time, don't set norms and limits, adolescents turn to drugs and alcohol to fill the emptiness."
-- Carrell Dammann, psychologist

The rise of the two-career couple spelled doom for family life. Typically Dad went to his office, Mom went to hers, and the kids went to school and then day care. The industrial revolution finally drove each member of the family into a separate factory system with rows of similar people doing similar things. *Ugh!*

Getting women to stay home is not the solution to family disintegration. Re-integrating or blending family and work as in the pre-industrial era seems to me a more "natural" solution.

Boundless

They talk about a woman's sphere
As though it had a limit;
There's not a place in earth or Heaven,
There's not a task to mankind given,
There's not a blessing or a woe,
There's not a whispered yes or no,
There's not a life or death or birth,
That has a feather's weight of worth--
Without a woman in it.

An Idealized Work/Family Solution for Today's World: Florence Griffith Joyner's family.

What does a blended family look like in today's world? The best example I came across in my interviews was the Joyner family.

Florence "Flo Jo" Griffith Joyner's success is indisputable. In 1988 alone she won three gold and a silver medal at the Olympics. Her world's records in the 100 meters and 200 meters earned her the title "World's Fastest Woman." She's so far ahead of the pack that she comes in first and her long, flowing, black hair comes in second.

Al Joyner and Florence Griffith Joyner work together as Olympic athletes, internationally recognized public speakers, owners of a designer nail company and founders of a charity for disadvantaged kids.

Although they are a *four* career couple they have no nanny. You heard it right: no nanny. They work together on everything they do and they almost always keep their daughter with them.

They train one another at the track while Mary, their five-year old plays in the sand, runs, or rides her bike. They take her along to speeches at corporations, associations and charity groups. In their home office Mary has her own computer and works on phonics or math.

School could be the one thing that eventually divides them. But for the time being, Flo-Jo devotes about two and a half hours each day teaching her daughter one on one in addition to the computer courses Mary does independently.

Okay, at this point, most people are probably shaking their heads thinking: "They are very lucky and have an unusual life. It has nothing to do with me. I can't do that."

Before you dismiss this image of family life as eccentric, stop and think about it. Does it make any less sense than the traditional Mom at home and Dad at work model? Does it make any less sense than Mom and Dad as corporate executives with the kids at God only knows where?

The lifestyle the Joyners have created is less a freak accident than it is an ideal. It is an extreme opposite of our modern culture in which families live together yet lead totally separate lives.

With all their money, choices, and the demands on their time and energy, it would have been easy for the Joyners to set up a lifestyle more like a two career couple with separate trainers, speaking schedules, and a nanny. It would have been easier for Flo-Jo to send Mary to school so that she could do her photo shoots and magazine interviews in peace.

Instead, they have made choices to work together, to be patient with one another, and to enjoy getting to know one another. If you think they are just lucky, you're dreaming.

We have a surprising ability to create the kind of success we imagine, so changing your image of success from two corporate jobs to a career that allows the family to be a team will change your life. What I want to do is change the paradigm of modern-day success from the two career couple to the way the Joyners live.

> "Beauty does not lie in the face. It lies in the harmony between man and his industry."
>
> -- Jean Francois Millet

Although the details of how you organize your life may look nothing like the Joyner family style, you can implement certain principles that make your family more like a team instead of a game of tug of war. In the rest of the book we'll cover lots of modern day variations of families that work as a team. It can be done in so many ways.

What is really exciting about being alive today is that new technology and the decline of manual, factory-based jobs gives us the opportunity--now more than ever--to return to a lifestyle much more like the pre-industrial community.

Even better, our lives are much easier, cleaner and healthier than they were 270 years ago. Whereas 75 percent of Americans had to be farmers in 1776, today less than 4 percent work in agriculture. Whereas in 1900 almost 60 percent of the work force went to factories, today it is less than 25 percent. We no longer have to work on farms and in factories.

Today, we can choose our vocation in a way never possible for Americans before us. Today, the vast majority of us are much freer to develop our minds, bodies and spirit through our work. You can find jobs creating pictures, stories, or ideas. You can get paid to work for your beliefs in the political arena, the religious world, or in the extensive non-profit sector. Or, like the Joyners, you can earn a living as an athlete.

Not only can you choose work that is fulfilling, but also flexible. Unlike farmers and factory workers, you can choose whether to live in cities or in the country. You can work in homes, in offices, on the road or, as Paul Zane Pilzer does, in a Jacuzzi or on a ski lift. And best of all, families can work together. What an amazing age we live in!

> You have got to know what you want,
> or someone is going to sell you a bill of goods
> somewhere along the line
> that can do irreparable damage
> to your self-esteem,
> your sense of worth, and
> your stewardship of the talents
> that God gave you.
>
> -- Richard Nelson Bolles

It may take many years of dedication and sacrifice to get to your ideal situation, but it is possible. After all, it takes years of dedication and sacrifice to create the kind of two-career success that can destroy our lives. *Before you spend your life working for an ideal of success, make sure it is what you want.*

After a hundred or so years we have come full circle from the industrial revolution back to an age where we can live and work at home with our families under one roof. At last count, more than 25 percent of the work force had a home office in which they work full or part time.

My paradigm, however, goes much deeper than whether or not you have a home-office. Although working at home may help the family feel included, some people with a home-based business still keep work and family quite separate. True blending creates a family team with a common goal.

At the same time, a home business that involves the whole family 100 percent may not be necessary. You can still build a team spirit in your family if you work outside the home. Not everyone will want to start a home-based business with a spouse and then employ the kids. It isn't necessary.

What is really necessary to create a highly blended work and family life in the modern world? What are the building blocks?

As I interviewed my role models certain principles emerged repeatedly, not because I asked, but because they brought it up. Those who were succeeding sane with kids couldn't talk about their success without talking about their kids. Family and work didn't fit neatly in different worlds; the lines were blurred. My role models were blending work and family.

The common elements among the lives of high flyers with healthy families added up to a very different vision of success than what I had absorbed growing up. For example, I believed husbands and wives shouldn't work together.

Corporations where I have worked usually have explicit or unstated policies to keep spouses as far apart as possible. Feminism gave me a sense that a woman who works with her husband will be overshadowed or dominated by him; she needs her own space. Couples who could and would work together seemed eccentric or quaint.

Similarly I had the idea that family life needed its own space. Bringing work home meant someone was a workaholic and didn't know how to balance. Quality time, as I understood it, was supposed to be free from work concerns. The philosophy of blending as I saw it practiced shattered all my unconscious assumptions about work and family.

What I saw among families of highly successful people was that families can and should work together. They used to do only that before factories became the norm. If a couple can't treat one another with respect and support perhaps they should work on their relationship until they can. Why else do we marry, if not to be treated as a respected partner?

For me, learning about the philosophy of blending was a process of stripping away a lot of unconsciously held assumptions about work and family. When I put these assumptions in historical perspective, I realized that many were based in the nature of industrial work: Splitting up families, creating narrowly focused work, measuring efficiency, and devaluing quality of life.

By giving up these assumptions I became free to design my life to meet my own standards in which I could work more like the village baker than like a factory worker.

"I never suspected that
I would have to learn how to live--
that there were specific disciplines
and ways of seeing the world
I had to master before
I could awaken to a
simple, happy and uncomplicated life."

-- Dan Millman

Principle #1

Your Family's Sanity Starts with You.

Susan Taylor, editor in chief of a national magazine for African American women with 7.3 million readers, wrote an entire book about her own experience of putting more sanity into her nutty life as a New York executive. Ah, New York, New York! If you can stay sane there, I guess you can do it anywhere.

"Most days I used to come racing home from the office completely stressed out," Susan Taylor writes in *Lessons in Living* (available from Anchor Books, Doubleday). "I'd hit the door, step out of my heels and head straight to the kitchen to start dinner, fussing at my daughter all the while: 'Turn off that television! Where is your homework? Did you clean up your room?'"

> "How we feel is not the result of what is happening in our lives,
> it is our interpretation of what is happening."
>
> -- Joseph McClendon and Anthony Robbins from Unlimited Power: A Black Choice

"One evening a friend of mine from out of town came home with me after work. After witnessing my madness, he asked if that was how I came home to Nequai every day. Well, I gave that brother fever. I told him I was raising my daughter the way my parents had raised me and I'd turned out just fine thank you. I went on and on. But I heard him.

"And over time I started coming home from work differently. After hugging and kissing my Pumpkin, I'd ask her to excuse me while I took a few minutes to restore myself. In our small, one-bedroom apartment, I retreated to the quiet of the bathroom to sit still for a moment.

"There I would remind myself to leave the pressures of work at work and to come back to my center. I'd remind myself not to scream and holler, but to be gentle and loving. Before cooking and correcting, I learned to just sit with Nequai for a few minutes and ask her about her day.

"At first she found it strange that I was even interested. But soon she began to trust my new behavior, and positive changes began to occur in our household. Perhaps for the first time, I felt happy and calm in the evening. I began to look forward to the time for nurturing and rekindling the love within our home. And Nequai grew calmer and happier, too. In time she went from being a failing student to becoming an honor student and eventually the valedictorian of her high school class."

In contrast to Susan Taylor, most people are unwilling to take personal responsibility for the insanity of success. Almost everyone says,

"You don't understand how it is in my field." No matter what their occupation, they feel it requires insanity.

"Computer programmers have to work all night, seven days a week to meet a deadline," I have been told. "Triathletes need total dedication," others say.

The medical profession, politics, business, Olympic competition, and almost every line of work has its own crazy demands. Many speaking professionals with whom I work are divorced because of all the travel required. No profession makes it easy to succeed and stay sane.

My role models for combining success with personal fulfillment were people who carved their own path to the top of their profession. They were not afraid to do things differently. They questioned the accepted wisdom in their field about the road to excellence. They looked for creative ways to achieve results using their unique resources. They dared to be different.

> "If you feel warm and comfortable you probably are in the middle of the herd."

Blending work and family in a way that nurtures both doesn't happen to anyone by accident. It starts with a decision to live by a different philosophy. It takes many years of making tough decisions, going against the crowd, and being a very creative problem solver. All of my role models wrestled actively throughout their careers with these issues. To me this seems like no great sacrifice. As a working parent you will struggle anyway. You will do hard work, make difficult decisions and become a creative problem solver.

"A man must learn to endure patiently that which he cannot avoid conveniently."

-- Michel De Montaigne

"Endurance is often a form of indecision."

-- Elizabeth Bibesco

Yet without the blending philosophy, parents can end up ten years down the track in a position of great suffering. I have concluded that since you have to do the hard work anyway, you might as well aim for a blended lifestyle.

The first principle, therefore, can be summed up as making a decision to pursue the philosophy of blending. Blending is not the result of luck, picking the right career, or doing one easy thing. If you want a flourishing career and a strong family, it has to start with your decision to pursue a blended lifestyle.

> I decided long ago
> Never to walk in anyone's shadow.
>
> If I fail
> or I succeed
> at least I live as I believe.
>
> --Whitney Houston
> "The Greatest Love"

What You Can Do Now
to Be a Source of Sanity

Do you take responsibility for your sanity? Do you blame others for your lack of calm?

How can you add a few moments of serenity to your family's routine each day?

As you continue reading and applying the blending principles, you will find ways to increase your sanity.

Principle #2

Make decisions jointly as a couple or as a family.
The second principle that was common to families of high achievers was making decisions together.

When I was growing up we had family meetings that we called the Five Flags meetings. We kept the minutes in one of those hard bound, blank books. Topics included a costume for the school play or a sleeping bag for the Boy Scout camping trip as well as why the house was messy, or who was using whose towel.

> "In the new economy,
> individuals at all levels of the company
> and in all kinds of companies are challenged
> to develop new knowledge and
> to create value,
> to take responsibility for their ideas,
> and to pursue them as far as they can go."
> -- Alan Webber
> (in the Harvard Business Review)

Every week we started out the meeting by asking for agenda items. "Is there anything anyone wants to bring up?" the note taker would ask. Almost every week someone would say, "Yes, last night's dinner!" and then pretend to barf. We laughed and laughed, because at ten years old that joke is still funny week after week.

We were not adults, but the meetings served an important purpose. We all voiced our needs and solved our problems together in those weekly Five Flags meetings.

Not all families, however, do it the same way.

Lebron Morgan, an advertising executive for BET network, has what he calls the Board of Directors for Morgan, Inc. Whenever there is an important family decision to make like relocating or changing jobs, Lebron takes it to the board.

"The Board of Directors includes my lawyer, my accountant, and several of our respected family friends. But my daughters, my wife and I each have a vote on the Board, too."

In all the interviews where the subject came up, it was clear that the sanest families had some mechanism for making decisions together. It may not always be a democracy, but everyone was asked for their opinion, listened to, and taken into account in the process.

"Who of us is mature enough for offspring before the offspring themselves arrive? The value of marriage is not that adults produce children but that children produce adults."

-- Peter de Vries

"It takes more courage to reveal insecurities than to hide them,
more strength to relate to people than to dominate them, more 'manhood' to abide by thought out principles
rather than blind reflex.
Toughness is in the soul and spirit,
not in the muscles and an immature mind."

-- Alex Karras

What You Can Do Now
to Use Joint Decision Making

Do you give your kids a chance to express their opinions, solve problems, and voice their needs?

Ask others whom you respect how they make family decisions.

What is the next big decision coming up? How will you handle it?

Principle #3

Encourage all family members to explore and develop their passion, their skill and their personality through their work.

> "I yam what I yam."
>
> -- Popeye

Traditional roles can be a trap for both men and women. In some traditional families men are forced to work in jobs they hate to support the wife doing what she loves: being with children, cooking and decorating the house. In other traditional families the wife feels trapped at home while the husband loves his job and basks in praise and success.

The particular roles don't matter nearly as much as whether or not the individuals are growing and stretching themselves. Is everyone in your family happy with their jobs?

On the surface, David Alexander has a very traditional marriage. David stays busy being the President of Claremont College and the American Secretary for the Rhodes Trust, as well as holding numerous positions on boards and charities. His wife, Catherine, has devoted her time and energy to a career as a homemaker, raising their three children and keeping the house running.

> "Organizations intent on building shared visions continually encourage members to develop their personal visions."
>
> -- Peter Senge
> author of *The Fifth Discipline*

What keeps the Alexanders sane, however, is their ability to work closely as a team. She used her skill as a homemaker and a mother to support his role as President of the college. In their home she entertained students, faculty, parents, donors and visiting dignitaries. "One year we counted and found that we had invited over 3000 people as guests between January and November," David told me.

In addition to entertaining in their home, Mrs. Alexander built relationships that supported her husband's work by joining community organizations, getting to know students, and working with the officers of the college on fundraising events.

"We both felt we had the same job," says David. "I finally convinced them to give her a salary. It was small, but at least it recognized how hard she worked to manage the social life of the college."

Teamwork in their marriage went both ways. As an academic David was able to participate more in the family life than the traditional "Dad-at-work." He could frequently work at home or spend time walking around campus with his wife and children.

Contrast this picture with the traditional marriage in which Mom has no life outside the home and Dad has no role in domestic affairs. The Alexander's have only one career outside the home, but they share everything.

Encouraging everyone to develop their skills through work doesn't mean every couple has to have two careers. You can keep or toss out the traditional husband and wife roles. It doesn't matter. What matters is being able to work as a team supporting each other in their vocations.

What matters is that all are allowed to use their skills for something they love to do.

> "When you reach for the star in you, and in others, you'll see the limitless possibilities for success."
>
> -- Mary Ellen Drummond
> President, Polished Presentations

So before you turn to your spouse and propose a joint business involving the kids, ask yourself and ask your family about what sort of work they love to do. You may have to work separately building your expertise and reputation in your own fields before you can find a way to work together. Without igniting each person's individual vision and purpose, you don't get a deep commitment to the team.

For example, I will never succeed in getting my husband to quit being a physicist and manage my career as a speaker/author. He'd be damn good at it, but he loves physics too much to quit. And I love him too much to divert him from his true purpose.

At the same time, we have succeeded in finding a patch of common ground by starting our own computer consulting business alongside the other things we do. Grant has a prodigious skill with computers; I can program well enough to help.

> "My vision is not what is important to you. The only vision that motivates you is your vision."
>
> -- Bill O'Brien, CEO of Hanover Insurance

As I began my own business speaking and writing, he gave me ample computer resources, system management, and even wrote programs to streamline my fax marketing and my accounting system. Later we collaborated on a product we call "PC Soul Food," which gives you inspirational messages and ideas from *Succeeding Sane* throughout the day as you work on your computer.

Thus, although neither one of us expects the other to give up a career, we find ways to collaborate and support one another using our unique talents.

Having written this, and looked at many other examples, I am realizing I need to find more ways to support Grant in his primary work, his physics.

Although we will talk more about forming a team in the principles to follow, the point of this principle is that the individual passions, interests, and talents are more important than the team. Do not force individuals to fit the team...make the team fit the individuals on it.

> "The key to all motivation is desire and the master key is responsiveness to the needs, desires, and interests of the people you would lead."
>
> -- John Noe

"Pursue your own dreams.
Not your mother's, your lover's,
or your best friend's."

-- Walter Anderson
author of *Courage Is a Three Letter Word*

"Whatever beauty or poetry is to be found
in my little book
is owing to your interest in and
encouragement of all my efforts
from the first to the last;
and if ever I do anything to be proud of,
my greatest happiness will be
that I can thank you for that,
as I may do for all the good in me."

--Louisa May Alcott, author of *Little Women*
(writing to her mother)

What You Can Do Now
to Encourage Individual Growth

Write down the name of each person in your family (including you).

What could you do to encourage each one as an individual? What question could you ask? What support could you give? Which experiences could you share?

Names   What to do

Principle #4

Involve Your Children in Your Work

Encouraging kids to get involved in their parent's work is a recurring pattern among those who succeed and stay sane.

Here are some examples that happened to come out in the interviews while I was asking other things.

- I met one of Bob Chappelle's sons because I sat in on a training course taught by Bob that happened to be attended by his son. I found out that he always involved his children in his work with the Saturn Corp. He gave his son a job washing cars for the dealership at age ten. Later he hired two of his sons as sales consultants.

- While on hold for Laura Tyson I was told that she was escorting her 13-year-old son to the internship office. She isn't too busy to get her son involved and learning about the White House.

- Lebron Morgan shows his daughters the process of selling advertising from the idea to the finished ad. He even takes them along on sales calls from time to time. Once on a sales call on the Disney Company, his daughter told the client, "Hurry up and give my Daddy the business so we can go to the park!"

- Ken and Marjorie Blanchard have been joined in their training and development institute by their son and daughter who work in training and PR, respectively.

- As we described in the opening story, Florence Griffith Joyner takes her daughter everywhere: to train at the track, to speeches, and to work in the office.

I used to resent the opportunities that the children of successful people had. "It's nepotism," I thought. I wished I had rich and powerful parents to show me the ropes, too. But now I know that involving children in work is the only hope that successful people have of knowing and being understood by their children.

Lennart and Ginny Palme, network marketing entrepreneurs, convinced their adult children to give up other career aspirations and get involved in their thriving business. Their daughter, Pam Koenig, described for me the impact it had on the closeness of her family.

"Prior to getting started with this business I talked to my family maybe once or twice a month," explained Pam. "There was a lot of distance between us. They are in Chicago and I am in California. I'd see them maybe once a year at Christmas, if that. It was hard. We were all involved in our own things."

Deciding to work together changed their family dynamics.

"By doing business together I'd say we talk at least three or four times each week," said Pam. "We meet in person at least three or four times per year at company functions as well as getting together to help each other provide training sessions."

Pam acknowledged, however, that not everyone would want to work with their kin.

"I have an incredible family," Pam confided. "These are people who I would choose to work with even if they weren't related, because I trust and respect them absolutely." Even so it took more than six years for her to decide to give up her career in corporate sales and join her father's business venture.

Pam went on at length describing the unexpected benefits of working with her family to grow their business. "We are planning to go to Thailand together this summer because our company has established operations there and we can begin recruiting distributors...so it is a tax deductible family trip! As IDN enters more countries around the world, our dream is to travel the world together."

Involving your children in your work can start when they are very young and last a lifetime. I remember collating papers for the classes my mother taught before I even knew how to read. Today, she still asks me to come to her school every year and give a motivational speech to the student body. She has always found ways to use my skills.

Involving your kids requires patience and sincere interest in them as independent people. Offer opportunities, but don't insist. Support and participate in their interests if you expect them to support and participate in yours. (Of course this goes for your spouse as well as your children).

Unfortunately there is no *guarantee* that supporting their interests will translate into support for yours. As Ken Blanchard commented, "Between the ages of 12 and 21, most kids want nothing to do with their parents. Our two kids were no different. So when it turned out that they both graduated from college at the same time and didn't have a job yet and weren't in love, Margie and I decided to take them with us on a trip around the world visiting our foreign affiliates. We thought it would be a great time to reconnect. It was! The bonding time made it possible for Scott and Debbie to imagine working with us."

Designating a day for "Taking your daughter to work" is a great start. But the lesson I learned from the successful people I admire most is that it goes a lot deeper:

- Take your children to work often.
- Bring work home and involve your children.
- Help them understand what you do.
- Find out how they would like to contribute.
- Use your work as an opportunity for them to learn, to achieve, and to help support the family.

Living this principle of involvement makes it much easier to work on the next principle: creating a family mission.

"Kids learn positive lessons by watching their mother operating in the outside world, taking action, exerting influence, making decisions and using their talents flexibly and creatively."

-- Ellen Galinsky
President of the Families and Work Institute
in New York City

What You Can Do Now to Involve Your Children in Your Work

Do your children understand what you do?

Do you take time to explain the process as well as the tasks?

Do you talk about why you do it?

Do you ask for help? For advice?

Can you find things for your kids to do that they will enjoy and feel proud about doing?

Whether your office is at home or elsewhere, do you have a space for them to work or play alongside you? Are your children welcome visitors in your office?

If they do not want to get involved, let it be. Get involved in their work instead.

Principle #5

Build your team spirit into a sense of mission in your family.

This is much easier to do if you are already living the three previous principles: making decisions together, supporting each other in your personal career directions, and involving your kids.

The pre-industrial lifestyle allowed families to work as a team in both their "career" and their "domestic" chores. If the farmer needed help with planting or harvesting, you can bet the whole family was out in the field. If the baker's wife needed to go to market, she probably could leave the baby asleep in the crib while Dad was home. Of course, the exact nature of the team would depend on the individual marriage, personalities, and skills involved.

This order of things seems much more natural and healthy for a family than sending off every member in completely different directions every morning. You may be slaying dragons or fulfilling your sense of purpose at work, and then come home to strangers who have no idea how great you really are.

Your children and spouse should feel a sense of pride in what you do...and vice versa. If possible, they should even contribute to your work in some way and thus feel personal pride as part of the team. Ask them if there are ways in which you can contribute to their projects as well.

At the highest level, the entire family feels a sense of identity with your work in the way that the family name used to be the family profession: Mr. Baker, Mr. Miller, Mr. Smith. Your family profession was the outlet for demonstrating not only your skills, but also your values such as quality, commitment, reliability and teamwork. You could hold your head up high in the village if you belonged to a family known for quality workmanship.

The best example I came across of a family with a mission is Michael Osheowitz, my friend and mentor from Wall Street. He combined his passion for helping disadvantaged kids with his Wall Street job by starting an organization called "Sponsors for Educational Opportunity (SEO)" that helps minority kids get jobs in banking.

When involvement with the program began to take so much time that it conflicted with his job, he found a new job at an investor relations and financial consulting firm. By sharing his vision and passion, he convinced the partners at Arthur Schmidt & Associates to take on SEO as a pro bono client, thus allowing him to combine his charity work with his financial consulting. The arrangement worked so well that Osheowitz was able to work his way up to President of Arthur Schmidt & Associates and still keep SEO growing and maturing.

"One of my only regrets, as I look back, is that my attention was too much in the finance work and the SEO work," Michael mused. "I thought I was doing so much better than my peers because I came home early and stayed home on weekends. I thought I was such a good dad. I didn't realize I wasn't there mentally. I was preoccupied." (It was suggested that I leave this quote out because it undercuts the story. I leave it in to make several points: a) nobody's perfect. b) don't make the same mistake. c) be willing to admit your mistakes.

Even so, his family shared his passion for helping SEO kids. SEO kids came over for dinner and conversation at the Osheowitz home. Michael's daughters began with clerical work at the center in their teens and helped students, as they got older. Melita, a talented artist, taught art classes for students for a time.

Michael's wife was also very involved. Maria became so absorbed in helping youth through SEO that she gave up her career as a fashion designer and went back to school for a masters degree in clinical social work. Then, when SEO's executive director resigned without warning, Maria stepped in to fill the gap. She stayed on as executive director for more than two years, bringing SEO to a new level of institutional development and particularly strengthening the mentoring program.

"My first instinct was to try to help the kids. I had so much training and experience in social work. However, I saw that I could accomplish much more by bolstering the mentor program. Instead of stepping in to help kids, I steered them back to their mentors. I gave the mentors the support and encouragement to help the kids themselves.

"By example and by direction, I helped the SEO staff to put in the time and energy to make the mentoring relationships work instead of letting the kids rely on SEO staff directly. In the short run, it's easier to just deal with a child's problem. But in the long run the mentoring relationships make our load lighter and provide far more for the kids."

Maria not only formalized and strengthened the mentoring relationships but also the structure and professionalism of the organization itself. From letter writing and phone skills to handling serious psychological and emotional crises, Maria instituted procedures and training that brought the organization to a new level of effectiveness without losing its family feeling. Maria brought her unique strengths and abilities to the organization her husband had founded.

"Why did you leave?" I asked. "At first I grew a lot in the job as executive director. I suddenly went from being a graduate student to the representative of an important organization; it was good for me." Maria told me about meeting with major sponsors, making difficult decisions and other challenges she faced.

"After awhile, however, I felt that it was taking me off course. I did not want a career as an administrator. I wanted to work with kids directly as a clinical social worker. The longer I stayed at SEO, the harder it would be to establish a private practice. I was glad for the time I spent as executive director at SEO, but I love my work healing the wounds of children."

Each member of the family has contributed to the family mission of helping disadvantaged youth. Over the years many dinner conversations involved the entire family in major strategy issues or trying out new ideas. The whole family feels proud of SEO and feels some sense of identity that is based on the "family business."

Yet each person is still allowed to blossom individually. Today Maria has found her own calling as a psychologist for troubled teens in her own private practice. One of her daughters is working toward a degree in social work while the other works as an interior designer.

Michael has retired from being the president of the financial consulting firm and accepted a position as president of the foundation that supports SEO and two other programs for disadvantaged youth. "My life revolves around my family and the foundation," he says simply.

Not every family mission, however, will be a charitable cause. Most family missions revolve around one or both parents' chosen vocation. Don't forget...SEO isn't just social work. It is also about recruiting, mentoring and placing kids in Wall Street and other fast track jobs. At its core, the Osheowitz family mission is anchored in Michael's profession.

Whether your personal mission is mind-based, body-based, or spirit-based, it can involve the whole family and be an expression of your values. Let me give you a variety of examples to drive this point home.

Florence Griffith Joyner's family mission centers on hard work and excellence in running. It also supports a charity to help disadvantaged young athletes.

The Tyson-Tarloff family mission (described in the section on pacing yourself in Principle #6) centers on curiosity. This family observes and advises the world from the perspective of a journalist and an economist.

As senior executives for *The People's Network,* Lisa and Eric Worre have a family mission. They not only work in the same company, but they share a passion for what TPN represents: positive, empowering television programming available in your living room. Together they pursue careers, raise their kids, and change thousands of lives for the better. As a faculty member I have worked closely with them and see the sheer joy they find through work.

Many speakers and writers like myself have turned their job into the family business. Dottie Walters, a motivational speaker and author of many books, has brought her daughter, her husband, and even her grandson into her speaker's bureau business. Her mission to develop more teamwork and professionalism among speakers throughout the world has been taken up by her entire extended family!

Husband and wife teams abound among speakers who succeed and stay sane. Tony Robbins travels with his wife Becky who introduces him on stage. Olympian Bruce Jenner has his career as an inspirational speaker and author managed by his wife Chris.

Dr. Marjorie Blanchard is the President of Blanchard Training and Development founded by her husband Ken Blanchard, author of the *One Minute Manager.* They have co-authored a book, raised a family, and shared their work as corporate teachers in the fullest possible way.

> "Never one thing and seldom one person
> can make for a success.
> It takes a number of them
> merging into one perfect whole."
>
> -- Marie Dressler

To sum up, living up to principle #5 means becoming a tighter, more deeply committed team. To some people a team may be simply a loose confederation of people who live together and help one another. Creating a sense of family mission is different in two important ways.

First, the entire family is working toward a shared goal. They are creating something together. Rather than dealing with one another on a quid pro quo basis or "I scratch your back, you scratch mine," the family has a shared passion to do something together. Can you pool your skills and passions with your significant other to create a joint venture?

Second, it usually involves values or a contribution to society rather than just making money or surviving.
- Ask yourself this question: If you applied your core values to every aspect of your daily work, would you do anything differently?
- Another good test of whether you have incorporated your values into your work is this: Imagine your children following you through an entire week of your work. What would they learn about your values?

A good family mission is based on the passion of one or more members of the family and draws on the skills and enthusiasm of all. It could be art, music, business, food, medicine, travel...whatever.

Usually a vocation is raised to the level of a family mission with the addition of the family's particular values, desire for excellence, or the desire to help others.

"Shared vision fosters risk-taking, Learning can be difficult, even painful. With a shared vision, we are more likely to expose our ways of thinking, give up deeply held views, and recognize personal and organizational shortcomings."

-- Peter Senge
author of *The Fifth Discipline*

What You Can Do Now
to Develop a Family Mission

Do you have a project to work on as a couple or a family?

If not, try something small to start. Paint and redecorate a room in the house, work on the garden, take a class together, or plan a family vacation. Practice using joint decision making, tapping the interests of individuals, and involving everyone. Try to pick something where you can all feel you've achieved something.

Eventually you can work your way up to collaborating on a career-oriented goal. Ultimately you may reach the ideal of having an ongoing, major family project that is an expression of your values. Don't try to rush it. Just encourage it to grow.

Principle #6

Pace yourself.

> "Nothing valuable can be lost by taking time."
>
> -- Abraham Lincoln

Among all the people I interviewed for *Succeeding Sane*, Laura Tyson was sailing closest to the edge. As the first woman to head the White House Council of Economic Advisors since its inception in 1946, she had a crazy, high-pressure job in one of the most insane, high-pressure places in the world.

Yet, when I worked with her I sensed the calmness and sanity she carried with her down the halls of the Old Executive Office Building, in press conferences and into cabinet meetings in the Roosevelt Room. I looked up to this woman who looked elegant, handled difficult economic issues with ease, and kept a smile on her face most of the time.

I interviewed her while she still worked in the White House. My first question in the interview was, "What keeps you sane?"

"Spending time talking with my husband, Eric Tarloff, and my son, Eliot, about the right balance," she responded immediately. "Balance has always been an important issue in my life. But it never gets solved at the global level. Balance only gets solved day by day."

Neither my husband nor my son had their heart set on leaving Berkeley and moving to Washington DC. When I was offered the job of leading the Council of Economic Advisors, it came as a surprise to me, too. It was like this magical gift bestowed upon me."

The Tyson-Tarloff family talked it over. Eric's attitude was, "We've gotta go and do this because it's just too good an opportunity to pass up." That set the tone of moving to DC as a big family adventure. From the very beginning, they were all in it together. Mission? To learn, to stretch their wings, and to have a lot of fun and excitement.

Even with a clear mission, staying sane on a day-to-day basis in the White House isn't easy. "I am very conscious," Laura emphasizes, "of trying to get close to the right balance, but feeling that I have never actually achieved it. There are not many women at my level who have young children at home. For those of us who do, it is almost impossible to find time for something other than work, child and family. In the three years I have been here, I have never found a way to go to the gym during the week days."

You might think that Laura's life sounds a lot like that of the two career couple at the beginning of the book. Every moment of life is reengineered to maximize work hours and kid time with no time for personal sanity. Laura Tyson, however, has made some decisions about pacing herself that soften the blows from her fast-paced job.

First of all, she only has one child. Knowing her own work ambitions, she limited herself to one child with whom she enjoys quality one-on-one interaction. They go to science fiction movies or take Eliot's friends to a science fiction store on the weekend. On weeknights Laura may pass up an invitation to dine at an embassy in favor of having dinner at home and doing homework with her son.

"Those things help me refill my spiritual tanks," she said. "Someday I would like to have more involvement with children. I'd work with a group like the Children's Defense Fund so that I can help more of the world's vulnerable kids. But for now, one child is all I can handle."

> "The secret of happiness is not found in seeking more but in developing the capacity to enjoy less."
>
> -- Dan Millman

Another way that Laura paces herself is by guarding her weekend and evening time. "[As a top White House official] you can go out every night to great events: dinners, benefit concerts, speeches. You can see the right people and be seen. You can make trips around the world if you want and go to wonderful conferences and meetings. You can network, transact business, and develop your image. I realized I had to make a choice between having any personal life at all and doing those things."

Her solution is worthy of Solomon himself. She decided her basic commitment was to come home after work, do homework with Eliot, eat dinner, and be with her husband.

If, however, her husband who is a freelance writer and political commentator was interested in going to a really fun event, they hired a baby-sitter and went out.

"If he wants to go, I am happy to go. If he doesn't want to go, I am happy not to go." She shrugs her shoulders at the simplicity of it. "I rarely do things he doesn't enjoy, unless I am required to go as the speaker, for example." As a result she goes to the best, most interesting events with the full support of her husband, and enjoys most other evenings at home.

Perhaps the most important way in which she paced herself is that she didn't expect to live this way forever. Our conversation was peppered with references to a saner lifestyle in the past as an academic and with references to how she expected life to be different in the future.

"A university life allows more flexibility. There were more hours in a day that were not devoted to work." Although Laura won awards for her teaching, earned tenure for her research, and founded the Berkeley Roundtable on International Economics, she still found time for a dance class four times a week and driving in the car pool for Eliot and his friends.

"Here [in the White House] the work takes up more of my time and attention than I would like. I don't think it is sustainable. It is a tremendous opportunity with tremendous costs. You can only do it for awhile." Laura knows that having it all doesn't necessarily mean having it all at once, all the time.

Ken Blanchard taught me another lesson about pacing yourself, which particularly helps me as a speaker and author.

"You travel over a million miles a year," I asked him, "How do you stay so close to your family?" I worry about this question a lot in my own life. "At the beginning of the year," he told me "Margie and I sit down with a calendar and mark off time to protect for us. Four weeks at Christmas, a week at Easter, and eight weeks in the summer and a couple of other weeklong breaks. The rest of the year can be very insane, but from the very beginning we decided to get away together for than four months of the year. It has helped our relationship with our kids a lot." The Blanchard's have a serious commitment to pacing themselves.

"I'm not sure that you can balance your life everyday," says Ken. "You have periods of insanity. You have to give yourself periods of sanity."

Laura Tyson realized that her stint in the White House was just a brief period of insanity in her life. "I am well aware of what you're not able to do: being active in charity work, exercising, or just taking a walk and seeing how beautiful the spring flowers are. Some people just forget about all that. I could see that happening to me if I wasn't married to someone like Eric."

From the very beginning of our conversation, Laura emphasized the importance of being-married-to-Eric for Succeeding with Sanity. "I didn't marry someone who was driven by ambition. Eric is an artist, who cares about creativity and cares about sensitivity and cares about human relations. I knew I was doing that when I did it. He is an anchor that pulls me back to another way of looking at life."

"It is easy to get caught up in all this," she says waving her hand. "It's a very heady experience. The press and the Congress treat you like you are something important; it can cause you to lose your bearings. You have to constantly relate to what you were before and what you will be again. It is important to have people around who help you do that."

I suspect that the same is true of many driven men who are balanced out by supportive, more spirit-oriented wives. All of the married men I interviewed expressed appreciation and admiration for their wives' role as a teammate.

The women in high profile positions who I interviewed, however, made it clear that they could not be who they are and do what they do without their supportive spouse. Johnetta Cole, for example, former president of Spelman College, talked for a long time about the role played by her husband who helps her slow down, relax, and keep perspective. Perhaps the women particularly appreciated that men do not traditionally play such a role.

Laura went on to describe how Eric helps her keep perspective. "We have developed some close friends in Washington mostly because Eric has more time in his life as a freelance writer. He has always made more time in his life for friends than I have. He invests more time in his relationships."

As a result Laura can go out to small dinners with close friends who don't give a hoot about her title or image. "That's great," she says laughing. "I find that a revival."

To succeed and stay sane Laura paces herself day by day and year by year. She has followed many of the other principles, too. You'll notice that joint decision-making, team spirit; cultivating humility is all part of her story. The fact that her husband works for himself made it easier to move across country and also allows him to take up some of the slack as she works harder than ever before.

Laura may be sailing close to the wind, but she is still at the helm. Laura gets my vote as a wonderful and inspiring example of succeeding sane!

To sum up the principle of pacing yourself, it is important to realize that blending is not the same thing as having it all. Trying to cram everything you would like to be or do into one year of living is nuts.

I take a longer term view of life with some years or seasons being more family oriented and others more career oriented. I like knowing that I can spend more time cooking and making jam in one season, then work long hard hours when my manuscript submission deadline approaches. Pace yourself for the long haul.

"Be not afraid of growing slowly.
Be afraid of standing still."

Chinese Proverb

"Superficiality is the curse of our age.
The doctrine of instant gratification is a
primary spiritual problem."

-- Richard J. Foster

What You Can Do Now to Pace Yourself

Are you trying to do too much, too fast? Are you taking on more kids, a bigger house, and more job responsibilities all at once?

More isn't always better, but less isn't always satisfying, either. Try evaluating yourself with these questions:

- How much career achievement is "just right" for you?

- How much family time is "just right?"

- Are you actually headed toward where you want to be?

- Can you give yourself more time to get there?

- If your organization penalizes you for the pace of your progress, can you find an organization or slight change in occupation more suited to your pace and direction?

Principle #7

Use technology to defend your home life, not invade it.

New technology such as faxes, beepers and cellular phones can make us more accessible than we want to be. You may be one of those people who never has a weekend or evening without constant interruptions from the office or client emergencies. Consider the following ideas for turning technology into sanity's ally.

"Once we get over thinking of work as a slave-factory job, mixing work and home is a very pleasurable experience," says Paul Zane Pilzer, an author, economics lecturer and president of a CD-ROM publishing house. He lives and works out of his 8,000 square foot home in Park City, Utah.

Often he returns business calls while sitting in his Jacuzzi looking over the ski slopes. "I turn off the jets so they won't know where I am." In winter, he uses a cellular phone during the 45-minute ski lift ride up his favorite trail.

Can you imagine having no stacks of paper in your home office and no ringing phone? His secretary, back at the ZCI Publishing, Inc. headquarters in Dallas, summarizes all of his paper mail and voice mail with email notes that he can read quickly and respond to. "I hate voice mail...it goes on and on!" says Paul. Using technology, he has insulated himself from a hectic office life.

"I'm very involved with my brothers and their children and my cousins. Because I have large houses in nice places, I encourage them to visit." In the evening as everyone cooks, talks, and plays, Paul may join in or sit off to the side receiving and sending more email. He loves working while surrounded by family and the smells of good food.

Paul has tried every home office idea in the book. He's worked out of his home since 1976 when he was an economics professor by night and a Citibank vice-president by day. Having built dozens of homes for himself since then, he has continually refined his ideas and incorporated the latest technology. His current home is wired with a network so that he can hook in his laptop from any room in the house. "People ask me about the kind of computer to buy for their office and I say, 'Put it in the kitchen. Trust me.'"

Day or evening, he'll interrupt his business routine to chat with his guests, and he finds their conversation invigorating and inspiring. "There's nothing more rewarding than having your family and friends rooting you on: 'How did things go? How was that interview?'" Technology can trap you or it can free you. It's your choice.

> "To keep our faces toward change and behave like free spirits in the presence of fate is strength undefeatable."
>
> -- Helen Keller

What You Can Do Now
to Defend Family Life through Technology

Investigate ways to get more freedom through technology. Would a laptop or a cellular phone let you work wherever, whenever you want to?

If you had more freedom, how could it help you to blend work and family better?

Are you willing to invest your own money to buy technology that will reduce your stress and protect your sanity?

What is it worth to you?

Read Paul Zane Pilzer's story again to get ideas for using technology as a buffer for your sanity.

Principle #8

Find an Organization that Supports Your Goals, Values and Family Life

For Russ Karlen, even being his own boss did not offer him an organization that supported his goals, values and family life. He told me that as a contractor for owners of big estates of an acre or more who needed landscaping, tennis courts, stables and pools, "I made good money but it was not a quality life.

"During the period between 1979 and 1983--before cellular phones--I would be beeped 40 times per day," he said, shaking his head with dismay. "Usually I would be on the freeway heading for my next job or to pick up a check to meet the Friday payroll for my 50 employees. The calls were never to thank me for doing a good job. It was always a problem; crisis management."

"I couldn't turn my beeper off because I had so many things going on. Some of the jobs we were doing were three and four hundred thousand dollar jobs. I was working 18 and 19 hours a day until 11 o'clock at night.

"For example, I agreed to meet people at 7 or 8 at night to pick up a check for $10,000 for finishing the decking or laying a pool or whatever we had completed. They would never be there because they wanted to go to the show or something. They always had something else to do.

"Since I still had to collect the money, I would come back at ten or eleven. I would go back at midnight if I had to, and get people out of bed because I still had payroll to make plus all the subcontractors to pay." Russ struggled every day to collect payments. "From the nicest people in the biggest homes you often get bad checks.

"It was crazy. Then banks started getting taken over by the FDIC. I knew every pay phone at every gas station in Orange County better than the phone company. I reported most of the phones that didn't work. I never had a weekend, never mind a vacation.

"They came out with those beepers that buzz instead of beeping. Eventually every time it buzzed my body would start shaking. I knew I had to do something.

"When I would get up in the morning I was not a happy person even though I was making almost a million dollars a year."

Today, Russ Karlen feels he has found an organization that lets him live the way he wants to and do work that is meaningful to him. Russ is a "Blue Diamond" executive for Nu Skin, one of the most well established, multi-level-marketing companies in the U.S. "I traded in my business suit for a swim suit," laughs Russ. His daily business life is quite different from when he headed his own company.

"My typical day? I get up in the morning, put my swimsuit on and go out on the beach or in my back yard by the pool--or on the golf course in Las Vegas--and start making phone calls. I can work from any of my homes by telephone and fax machine. I teleconference with people in all 19 countries.

"When it gets to be time for lunch, I can take my wife, Linda, to the country club," he says as if this is some sort of miracle. "Most people end up spending more of the quality time in their day, more of their waking hours with their secretary than they do with their wives. I get to take my wife to lunch!

> "I shall be telling this with a sigh
> somewhere ages and ages hence:
> Two roads diverged into a yellow wood; and I --
> took the one less traveled by
> And that has made all the difference."
>
> -- Robert Frost

"We took a two hour lunch the other day. We are building a house together and went looking at other houses for ideas." The thought of these long married, parents cruising around talking about their dream house in the middle of the day gave me a warm feeling inside.

"We get to spend quality time during the day, which you normally wouldn't do. We do it every day--early in the morning, at noon, at night. We are together all the time. My daughter has never seen me go to an office." This ideal of work is so different from the one that most of us were brought up to want.

"We work together as a team." Sometimes they work together giving presentations and traveling the globe to build relationships. Other times they split up. For example, Linda may provide leadership for the existing organization while Russ is opening new markets in Thailand or the Philippines.

Their daughter, Brittany, has been answering phones and speaking at meetings from the age of three.

"I was going to tell a story to introduce my eleven-year-old daughter at a meeting of over five hundred people, but she was already up on the stage trying to take the mike out of my hand." Watching her father address groups has given her a role model and made her comfortable doing what 75% of Americans say they fear more than death itself: public speaking. The older kids also speak at meetings, travel on business, and work with their parents.

"Of course, it's not perfect," says Russ, "Nothing is. We tell our daughter Brittany that Nu Skin arguments don't count because it is part of doing business. You don't always all agree on what direction you are going in. You have to make decisions as to whether you do this or that. But it's something you do together."

Even with the arguments and the work says Russ, "We still have more special time together than if I worked in an ordinary corporate job.

"Today every day is like a vacation because it is enjoyable. I make phone calls and know that just with a couple of calls I might motivate someone to be better today than they were yesterday. I may teach them something I have done right or wrong over the last ten years in network marketing.

"When I was introduced to this business someone told me, 'You can have the freedom to do what you want to do when you want to do it.'

"I didn't know what they were talking about. I thought freedom meant democracy: free speech and the right to vote.

I was tied to my beeper, I was tied to my business, I was a slave to my subcontractors, and I was a slave to my customers. I didn't have freedom. I didn't understand what freedom meant."

Russ now understands a new meaning of freedom. "Over the last five years my daughter's class has been reading out loud once a week and inviting the parents to come and listen. I am the only father that shows up; all the other fathers are at work. I can come at nine o'clock, ten o'clock, eleven o'clock...whenever. The other wives ask, 'What does he do that he can come?' I can move my schedule around the family. Most other people can't.

"My father was a doctor and lived in the emergency rooms," says Russ. "He ran the hospital. He lived for all the people who got injured in the world. Family came second. For a doctor, it had to be that way. In my business, family comes first."

Russ Karlen made a decision to get out of a business that held him hostage and start a new career that allowed him to put family first. Joining a network marketing company gave him the freedom he wanted.

Network marketing with a well-established company can offer a unique career structure that blends the advantages of self-employment with the advantages of a major corporation. Many people are finding that multi-level marketing in a high-tech, global company is a structure that supports succeeding sane.

You can choose products you believe in and people with whom you feel comfortable. Russ Karlen works with vitamins and skin care products. Other role models of mine such as Lisa and Eric Worre work in network marketing of motivational and educational books, tapes, and television programming through *The People's Network*. Total family commitment and a passion for their products helps make them successful at multi-level marketing.

For you, however, the right niche may or may not be in a network marketing company. Changing to a new corporation, changing your job title or simply changing your attitude may be what's right for you.

> You have to find yourself reflected in the place that pays your salary.
>
> -- Bonnie St. John

Perhaps the most compelling story of a search for the supportive organization is that of Bob Chappelle. As the owner-operator of a Buick dealership in Oregon, he gained a reputation as an eccentric: the honest car dealer. Car dealers thought he was too soft to stay in the business. Customers loved him.

When his "new" method of using integrity, openness and no-hassle showed promise, he began teaching others. Soon he had a second career traveling the country helping dealers to retrain their sales force and reorganize their selling system. Along the way he met Charles McLean, a Buick dealer in San Diego with a similar style and values. Charles had hired an all female sales force to underscore the promise of a friendly, hassle-free selling approach.

Many years later Charles told Bob about a new car company called "Saturn" that employed Bob's principles of honesty and integrity in everything they did. Every rule, policy, and idea supported the backbone of values from the way Saturn treated its employees to offering a 30-day, money-back guarantee for its customers. Bob could not only sell cars in a certain way, he could have the full backing of the car manufacturer.

Bob moved his family to San Diego and helped his friend Charles set up the first Saturn car dealership in San Diego. Although it was tough going the first few years with no cars available and no track record, the company's rise to $50 million in sales within five years is now the stuff of legends. The customers are on fire with a passion about the quality of the car as well as the integrity of the company.

Bob, the "softie car dealer," found a home.

> "The secret of all generally successful people is that they have found their paths."
>
> -- Donna Blaurock, *Cheat Notes on Life*

And his family shares his enthusiasm for the way Saturn works. At thirteen years of age his youngest son began washing cars for the dealership. His biggest problem then was not being able to drive the cars around to the front when he was done.

His next biggest problem was being too young for a work permit. Solution: He started his own business and let his father file a 1099 form with the IRS.

I didn't hear about Chappelle's son because I asked or because he makes a big deal about it. It just happened to come up. When I sat in on two days of Saturn's sales consultant training as part of my research for the book, Chappelle's son was attending the class, too.

Turns out that all of Bob's sons have become Saturn sales consultants. I don't know whether that says more about the company or the father. But I think they found a company that lets them live their mission: honest, fun, no-hassle car sales.

There are examples throughout this book of people who manage to find a niche that supports their family and values.

- Michael Osheowitz, the financial consultant, changed to a smaller, more flexible investment company.

- Susan Taylor, editor of a national magazine, changed her attitude to her work and home.

- Paul Zane Pilzer, CEO of his own CD-Rom company, decided to work at home and use technology as an ally.

It is up to you to change your organization or the way you fit into it such that your work supports your values and family life.

"One cannot build a learning organization on a foundation of broken homes and strained personal relationships...

Ironically conflicts between work and family may be one of the primary ways through which traditional organizations limit their effectiveness and ability to learn."

-- Peter Senge, author of *The Fifth Discipline: The Art and Practice of the Learning Organization*

What You Can Do Now
to Move Toward a Supportive Organization

Write down the characteristics of a job or a company that would be supportive of the goals, values and the lifestyle you want for your family.

Does such a company exist?

What could you do to get closer to this ideal?

- Could you discuss changes with your employer?
- Change companies or jobs?
- Start being more supportive of the values and needs of your subordinates?

Principle # 9

If you can't find a supportive organization, create one.

> "When you die and go to meet your maker you're not going to be asked: 'Why didn't you become a messiah or find a cure for cancer?' All you're going to be asked is: 'Why didn't you become you?'"
>
> -- Elie Weisel, *Souls on Fire*.

I decided to create my own job because I didn't see any career paths that did not penalize motherhood. I wanted a part-time job with unlimited potential for learning, promotions and salary growth.

When my daughter was about two months old I met up with a friend from my gym, Susanne. Susanne's daughter, Rachel, is three weeks older than my daughter Darcy. As we strolled through the park with our babies, I told her about the business I was building.

"I use my experience as an Olympic skier, a Rhodes Scholar, and a former White House official to motivate people," I explained. "I teach everyone from executives to disadvantaged children how to perform at world class levels in less than ideal conditions. They get excited by my story of triumph over disability and other obstacles. "

I told her that I needed someone to help with booking speeches, answering the phone, and handling the mail-- especially when I was on the road. I thought it would be a good opportunity for someone with a child who wanted a part-time, home-based job. If she wanted to do it, we could even share a nanny for the two girls.

Susanne was so excited about the idea she began work immediately and never once looked back.

Things began slowly at first because we had so little time to work. We both nursed our daughters for nine months and did the majority of their care. The physical, hormonal and mental toll left us with about fifteen hours of productive business hours in a week. At the same time I was hammering away on my first book. At that rate, it took us about a month to do what other entrepreneurs could accomplish in a week.

There were times when the babies were screaming, the nanny was sick and work felt like we were trying to empty a swimming pool using thimbles. Susanne, however, always believed in me and in the vision of what we were building for ourselves.

Today, two years later, I travel the country regularly speaking for conventions, business meetings and charities. We have launched audio, video and book products on teamwork, visioning, peak performance and leadership.

Though she still works part-time, Susanne has developed her knowledge, relationships and skill in the meetings industry. She negotiates contracts, handles all our marketing subcontractors, and manages the development of products. Although she started as an office assistant she has grown into the role of managing the business. Her title should be "Empress of the Office."

When I am on the road, I feel secure knowing that Susanne will help Darcy bridge any gaps between the nanny, Grant, or my mother. Darcy always has another home. Because Susanne has a daughter the same age I know she has diapers, medicines and all the right knowledge to handle any problems that may arise.

When I am home, I try to knock off work at about three in the afternoon and spend quality time with Darcy before dinner. If Susanne needs extra time in the office, I will take Rachel along with Darcy to the park or the mall. "It's like having twins with two mothers," I often explain, while pushing our double stroller.

When we started I knew it would be great to share the cost of a nanny and have the mutual support as working mothers. We still treasure all the obvious things like being able to have lunch with the girls, get hugs throughout the day, and take off entirely if they need us for an emergency. We have home offices at both my house and Susanne's, so we can choose to be close to the girls or farther away for uninterrupted focus on work.

Luckily, Susanne and I have similar values on mixing work and kids. The last line of our contract says, "The success of this Agreement will be judged not only by profits, but also by the *way* in which we do business and the *quality of our lives.*" We spend time on a day-to-day basis discussing our priorities and how to get the most enjoyment out of what we do. We create a supportive organization on a daily basis.

What I didn't plan for was how much the arrangement has benefited the girls. They get so much love and security from each other. Now that they can walk and talk, they greet each other with smiles and hugs in the morning.

When one is crying the other will either cry in sympathy or try to comfort the other. They also learn from each other about dancing, singing, neatness, and kindness. They learn to play together and share toys without having to go to a daycare center.

As I mentioned before, my husband is not going to quit being a scientist and head up my business as an author and speaker. So I have the next best thing: Susanne and Rachel have joined my work-family unit.

It feels like an extended family or a clan that includes Grant; Susanne's husband, Greg; my mother, who lives in San Diego, too; and our nanny, Alissa. Everyone contributes to the upbringing of the children. It's like the old saying, "It takes a whole village to raise a child."

I can't fully acknowledge here all the special things everyone in our clan contributes to our business venture, but I can give you the flavor of it. Grant designed a software product for us to sell, maintains our computer systems, and answers our ethical questions as chief sage. Greg, who owns a business consulting in the oil and gas industry, has lent his experience in business to help us with contracts, tax issues, and reviewing our financial projections and accounting.

My mother, who is my muse, my inspiration, and a hall-of-fame grandmother, contributes everything from critiquing manuscripts to designing play environments for the girls. Without her love and support, I most certainly would not be succeeding sane in the process of writing a book, speaking nationally and raising a child.

And our wonderful, gifted nanny not only enriches the lives of our daughters, she helps us by running errands, promoting seminars, and testing our material. As a college student learning to be a translator for the deaf, she has even shared my Laser Walk technique with deaf audiences.

We are truly blessed with a highly blended life.

To sum up this principle, imagining and creating the ideal organization for your situation can take many years of hard work. But why work your guts out for someone else when you can work to create your dream employer?

"Some of us have great runways already built for us.
If you have one, take off.
If you don't have one, then understand it is your responsibility to build one for yourself and for those who would follow you."

-- Amelia Earhart

What You Can Do Now
to Create a Supportive Organization

Is self-employment the only way you will be able to blend your skills, family and values?

Describe your ideal company and how it can support your ideal lifestyle while generating profits.

Principle #10

Focus your efforts and your relationships.

The last principle is about learning to let go of those activities and commitments that do not support the core thrust of your life.

You can't do everything for everybody. Volunteering for ten different charities or sitting on eight different boards is not a sign of a highly blended life. When you are infusing your work with your values and involving your family, you don't need ten different clubs to meet your needs.

> "The sage knows himself
> but makes no show.
> He lets go of that and chooses this."
>
> -- Lao Tsu
> from the Tao Te Ching

Having a family mission brings your professional life and your personal life into harmony. That's what allows you to focus. People you work with become family, and family pitches in with the work.

Those who work this way become very careful about the kind of people who they choose to let into their "family." At Southwest Airlines they used to interview about twenty people to fill one slot. Today they interview as many as fifty people for each opening.

"First and foremost we are looking for a sense of humor," Kelleher told *Fortune* magazine. Then we are looking for people who have to excel to satisfy themselves and who work well in a collegial environment. We don't care that much about education and experience, because we can train people to do whatever they have to do. We hire attitudes."

> ## "Self-discipline is self-caring."
>
> **-- M. Scott Peck
> author of *The Road Less Traveled***

At the same time, CEO Herb Kelleher treats his employees as his extended family or his clan. He laughs at CEOs who sit on a bunch of boards and hang out with other CEOs. "My people are the fountain of youth," says the man everyone just calls 'Herb.' "They are restorative and rejuvenating for me. I love to be around them."

Faith Popcorn, noted futurist and author of *Clicking*, identifies "clanning" as a major trend for the coming century. The need for a group and a sense of belonging is in part a reaction to the excess of individualism in the 70s and 80s. Yet, at the same time it is an expression of one's personality and choice of identity.

Be willing to cut down on (or eliminate) activities not intimately related to your group's mission. After retiring from his executive position at an investment banking firm,

Michael Osheowitz is looking to focus his memberships, board positions and other commitments. In addition to being President of the Edwin Gould Foundation, he is only willing to be involved with other businesses or non-profits that can actively collaborate and create mutual benefits.

"I really want to stay perfectly focused," he told me, "but it's always a struggle. It is always tempting to get involved in other projects with friends who are presidents of other foundations. They have ideas; they need help. But I am remaining true to my course: focus and collaboration."

> "Be brief;
> for it is with words as with sunbeams--
> the more they are condensed
> the deeper they burn."
>
> -- Southey

You, on the other hand, may not be ready to focus your life as much as Herb Kelleher or Michael Osheowitz, but you can keep it in mind as an ideal to which you will progress as your mission becomes clearer and easier to support.

Having a highly blended life doesn't mean trying to cram everything under the heading of one business. Select quality activities and people to keep close to you just as you would select high quality furniture in your house. Focus and be selective.

An essential difference between succeeding sane and crazy is being very clear on your mission and sticking to what matters...both personally and professionally.

> "Don't assume that being more successful means more clubs, more commitments and more relationships."
>
> -- Bonnie St. John

"Our life is frittered away by detail... Simplify, simplify."

-- Henry David Thoreau

"The power of a man increases steadily by continuance in one direction."

-- Ralph Waldo Emerson

What You Can Do Now
to Focus Your Efforts and Relationships

Make a list of all the clubs, professional organizations, boards, jobs and volunteer activities in which you are active.

Are all your activities pulling in the same direction? Does each activity contribute to the effectiveness of the others?

If the whole picture is not greater than the sum of the parts, you may want to clarify your mission.

Can some activities be integrated more closely with the main direction of your life? For example, the majority of my charity work is in the form of volunteer speeches. Thus, it helps the group and helps my speaking ability at the same time.

If an activity can't be integrated more closely to the core, can it be eliminated?

Conclusion: Do It Your Way

Peeking into the private lives of high-flyers while researching my book was an exciting adventure for me. I hope you, too, have enjoyed hearing these moving stories about how families can work together and learn from each other in the process.

The stories I have shared in this book gave me a new outlook on what being a working parent could and should be. Assumptions I didn't even know I had were smashed forever. I thought husbands and wives weren't supposed to work together. I thought family needed to be protected from the work of high achievers. I thought cooking dinner together and playing together was enough to cement a family. I saw living proof to challenge these assumptions.

In each family I saw the same basic lesson repeated: making more time to involve family in one's work allowed these super achievers to reduce the tension between work and family as separate goals.

How you do it is not important. There are a whole range of options between the two-career couple that both work for someone else, and the family-centered, home-based business. Among the role models presented in this book there are all kinds of jobs and all kinds of families.

What is important is not how you structure it, but rather how it feels. Beneath all the differences was a common vision of how a family could be loving, close and highly achievement oriented at the same time.

> ## How Blending Feels:
> When it feels like everyone in your family is included,
> you're on the right track.
> When it feels like everyone in your family is challenged to use personal skills to contribute to a common goal,
> you're on the right track.
> When work, family and values feel
> more in harmony than at odds,
> you're on the right track.
> When you eliminate all the extra things that make your life hectic without supporting your family mission,
> you're on the right track.

Through these ten principles of **Blending** you can create a tightly integrated and satisfying lifestyle. Of course it takes patience and long term commitment to improving in each area a little bit every year. By the end of five or ten years, one can imagine achieving a blissful, family centered success like that enjoyed by Ken Blanchard's or Florence Griffith Joyner's family.

Although you may not instantaneously find common ground between the separate lives you lead, the immediate results of blending are also worth having. You can find creative ways to get involved with one another's pursuits. You can use joint decision making, pacing yourself, and other principles to ease the tension between your separate lives and goals. You can open a dialog with your family on how to pool your talents.

The immediate benefit I treasure most is hope. I have a vision of a lifestyle that can give me everything I want out of life without causing me to have a nervous breakdown. Blending as a philosophy has given me hope that I can let loose my talents without sacrificing my family.

> "We know about remorse and death.
> But do we know about hope and life?
> I believe in life after birth!"
>
> -- Maxie Dunham

> "I will not follow
> where the path may lead,
> but I will go where there is no path
> and I will leave a trail."
>
> -- Muriel Strode

What You Can Do Now to Make Blending Work for Your Family

- Rate yourself on a scale from one to five on each of the ten principles for blending work and family.

____ Your family's sanity starts with you.

____ Make decisions jointly as a couple or as a family.

____ Everyone in the family develops their passion, their skill and their personality through their work.

____ Involve your children in your work.

____ Build team spirit into a family mission.

____ Pace yourself.

____ Use technology to defend your home life.

____ Find an organization which supports your goals, values and family life.

____ Create a supportive organization, if you must.

____ Focus your efforts and your relationships.

- In which areas do you need the most work?
- Photocopy the summary list of principles and the summary exercises from the pages that follow. Post them some-where and look at them frequently. Highlight a few and make them a priority.

Ten Principles for Sane, Successful Families

1) Your family's sanity starts with you.

2) Make decisions jointly as a couple or as a family.

3) Encourage all family members to develop their passion, their skill and their personality through their work.

4) Involve your children in your work.

5) Build team spirit into a family mission.

6) Pace yourself.

7) Use technology to defend your home life, not invade it.

8) Find an organization that supports your goals, values and family life.

9) If you can't find a supportive organization, create one.

10) Focus your efforts and your relationships.

SUMMARY OF EXERCISES
for
BLENDING WORK AND FAMILY

1) Your family's sanity starts with you.
How can you add a few moments of serenity to your family's routine each day?

2) Make decisions jointly as a couple or as a family.
What is the next big decision coming up? How will you handle it?

3) Encourage all family members to explore and develop their passion, their skill and their personality through their work. Think about each person in your family (including you). What could you do to encourage each of them to use their talents?

4) Involve your children in your work. Do your children understand what you do? Do you ask for help?

5) Build team spirit into a family mission.
Do you have a project that all of you can work on together? If not, try something small to start. Eventually you can work your way up to having an ongoing family project that is an expression of your values.

6) Pace yourself. Are you trying to do too much, too fast? Are you taking on more kids, a bigger house, and more job responsibilities all at once? Try to think about how much of everything you can handle at once. Taking on too much can sink your entire ship. How much of what you want in your life will make you happiest? How much is enough? Can you give yourself more time to get there?

7) Use technology to defend your home life, not invade it.
Investigate ways to get more freedom through technology. Would a laptop or a cellular phone let you work wherever you want to? Re-read Paul Zane Pilzer's story about his home-office design for more ideas.

8) Find an Organization that Supports Your Goals, Values and Family Life.
Write down the characteristics of a job or a company that would be supportive of your goals, values and the lifestyle you want for your family. What could you do to get closer to this ideal?

9) If you can't find a supportive organization, create one.
Do you really need to be self-employed? What would your company be like?

10) Focus your efforts and your relationships.
Take stock of your affiliations. Does each activity support the others? If not, can they be eliminated?

Acknowledgments

First and foremost I am grateful to the famous and successful people named in this book who took the time to be interviewed. They let me look behind the curtain to see their private lives behind their public success. It has changed my life forever.

In addition I would like to acknowledge that I could not be a writer or produce this book without support from the following people:

- All my established writer friends who took me in and treated me like a professional writer from the beginning. You know who you are, lunch bunch. In particular, I want to thank Beverly Trainer for unfailing support and Sylvia Tiersten for jumping in at the last minute with editing assistance. Angels do exist.

- Ruby, my mother, who was always there with a new idea or an article to banish writer's block; who took classes with me; who took Darcy away for the weekend when I needed to write; and who didn't balk at some of the things I wrote about. A rare mom, indeed!

- April, my sister, the only person who volunteered to do close, time-consuming editing at no charge. She loves books as much as I do.

- Wayne, my brother, who gave me the courage to become a writer by his example and creed: "a writer is a person who writes." I come from a family of writers.

- Susanne Scherman who kept me sane and successful by not only sharing my business responsibilities, but also sharing my life as a mother, a cook, and a gardener. She understood the concept of blending long before the book was written. (To Greg and Rachel: thanks for sharing her!)

- Grant, who bought a computer for me to write a book during the first year of our marriage. He always encouraged me--not to do what he thinks I should do--but to find out who I want to be. He supported me with every bit of skill, and every ounce of compassion he could give.

- Darcy, my daughter, who forced me to slow down the writing process, to think leisurely, and to feel a lot more. I am a better person for knowing you.

> "I hope life treats you kind,
> I hope you have all that you dream of,
> I wish you joy and happiness,
> But above all this, I wish you love."
>
> -- Dolly Parton
>
> (Sung by Whitney Houston
> for *The Bodyguard*)

Additional Products by *Bonnie St. John*

- ***Succeeding Sane: Making Room for Joy In A Crazy World (published by Simon & Schuster)***
Bonnie St. John – a disabled, African-American Olympic ski medallist, Rhodes Scholar, former White House Official and business woman – shares her personal formulas for making it to the top of your field without sacrificing the things most important to you.

- ***The Winner's Mind***
Unleashing Your Peak Performance - An audiotape to help you focus all your knowledge and energies so you can achieve your highest level of performance when and where you want it. You'll hear how to Bonnie has successfully applied this technique to win at the Olympics and how easily you can apply it to your professional career, sports and other areas where you need to perform under pressure. Easy step-by-step instructions.

- ***Teamwork Under Fire***
High Performance in Less Than Ideal Conditions - In this 45 minute videotape, learn how to build an effective team in the midst of minefields like downsizing, political crises, mutual distrust, or the restructuring program of the year. Bonnie will show how you can create an effective team when the players, issues, and loyalties are constantly changing.

To order any of our products or to find out more about Bonnie St. John, please write, call or surf:

St. John Deane, Inc.
315 S. Coast Hwy. 101, Suite U-94
Encinitas, CA 92024

e-mail bonnie@sjd.com
(760) 944-7590
www.sjd.com